COACHELLA ELEGY

Coachella Elegy
by Christian Gullette

Winner of the 2023 Trio Award

TRIO
HOUSE
PRESS

Gullette, Christian
1st edition

ISBN: 978-1-949487-22-0
Library of Congress Control Number: 2023945635

Interior design by Natasha Kane
Cover design by Joel W. Coggins
Editing by David Groff and Natasha Kane

Trio House Press, Inc.
Minneapolis
www.triohousepress.org

for Michael

TABLE OF CONTENTS

In Transit

Palm Springs

We drink Fernet by ironic sculptures
under misters that make our bangs damp.

It's our anniversary,
though that time feels faint.

We are searching for a place
to escape his diagnosis,

laws against gay marriage,
our leaky, flat roof.

Every Memorial Day
and Labor Day, we go to the desert.

Sometimes also the Fourth
of July.

Palm Springs rewinds things.
We almost buy that mid-century chair,

proud of our rule that love for it
needs to be immediate.

At the Parker, a guy with a calf tattoo
brings drinks.

You can ask for anything here.
We toast to another year without cancer.

After dinner, we wander the hotel hedge maze,
nowhere to go this late but home.

Re-Monarching

Butterflies overwinter
in the milkweed
along storm drains.

Scientists count fewer
every year —
this year, the fewest.

Had we been
here only five years
ago

we'd have seen hedges
full of wings
and black veins.

There's such
a thing
as butterfly music.

We'd have watched
them sunning,
felt their density

cluster,
between needles
of pincushion cacti

planted by the front door,
a runway
of concrete squares

illuminated at night.
Power-saving strips
solar activated.

The house isn't ours.
We nap in it
every afternoon

while the waterfall
spills
over the hot tub,

feeds the pool
as if from an unending
source.

Quake

He reclines on his elbows
beside the pool,

says they should abolish
the filibuster.

Fatigue, he says.
This is what they want.

The water is untroubled
after last night's tremor,

the epicenter
somewhere beyond
the highway.

The world
is coming apart.
Fire in the mountains.

He's next to me.
Depthless water,
his body uncovered.

Our drinks sweat
under the umbrella
and the fruit trees.

That evening,
another tremor.

We return to the Airbnb
to find oranges
in the still-warm pool.

Airbnb Art

Under a Sputnik-shaped lamp,
a Picasso with three eyes.

My husband's prosthetic eye
is as blue as the other.

After the surgery,
we had sex,

his eye under a gauze tent.

I injected lidocaine through a tube that
coiled behind the bandage.

I wiped his armpits
with a washcloth.

There were still traces
of a purple arrow

drawn by the nervous surgeon.

The ocularist hand-painted his pupil.
It looks like the eye I always loved.

Mid-Century Modern

Behind glass walls,
the host slices limes.

I'd follow L.A. boys anywhere.

One kneels poolside
with a tray of Jell-O shots,
his shoulders peeling.

Desert palms echo in Ray-Bans.
Another guy fidgets with the knot
in my swimsuit.

Without indoors or outdoors,
I can invite everything in.

By the searing, metal ladder,
memory is too hot
to climb out of.

My husband watches from a strip
of artificial grass.

In the desert,
you have big afternoons
not big nights.

Coachella Elegy

Somewhere there's music.
We drive by Coachella

to the Salton Sea.
A sea as dead as Salt Lake.

My phone buzzes.
It's the anniversary

of my brother's death.
There are no reeds

as there are at Cana
and this water will not

become wine.
Shorebirds drink it,

not because they love
the world

but because
there's a magnet in it.

Is that freedom,
this wandering?

There's a forgotten
swing set submerged

in this sea. Young people who
once swayed on it still exist.

Salt, I float in it,
wanting to be held up.

Experimental Orchard

Driving toward Sacramento,
he quizzes me on GRE words.
I need to learn at least ten
before we reach
the experimental orchard.
A repository of stone fruit
and walnut genes, persimmons.

In 1875, Albert Bierstadt painted
the Sacramento Valley:
California Spring
a fantasy with cows grazing empty vistas,
indigenous people excluded
from the canvas's expanse
of once-plentiful oak.

The oak ended up in new towns,
coastal ports.
On the way back to San Francisco,
with olives
and pomegranates,
my GRE practice score is the same.

In a museum,
California Spring hangs near a collection
of early chairs.
I remember movies with westward wagons
stuffed with chairs.

Palm Canyon Drive

On a hotel rooftop,
we survey a boulevard below
on its way

to an even smaller city
named after a cathedral,
not a specific one

but a cathedral city.
None of its spires are visible
from Palm Springs,

this hotel rooftop
that feels like the right one
tonight.

Balcony shields
keep our napkins
from flying away

but the plexiglass
is low enough
for a view

of lights
in the mountain pass
we drove through.

How could an ocean
be so close, we thought,
but also impossible?

This is every day
for people who live here
surrounded by wind turbines,

your hand
not casually on my thigh,
the start of a vacation

that's unmeasurable
since the DJ's tunes don't
ever fade out.

What we could call
our day's history
was (maybe?) an hour

downtown
in a store called Gay Mart
buying underwear.

No, the drink isn't lying to you,
we don't lose
these scenes

when we come
down to
street level.

Gadolinium (Gd)

Intravenous ions,
metallic complex for the MRI scan,

his body as I watch becomes an interstate
of dye-drenched veins,

contrast agent tracing
the melanoma gripping the back of his eye.

Whatever privacies there are in this body,
they are different than what he arrived with,

a body happening as I watch it,
microscopic spaces now paramagnetic,

coursing with gadolinium, one of the rare-earths
though I'm barely acquainted with the world

blurring before me. I pretend to understand these scans.
His brain looks like water

after rinsing a brush, or a night view from space,
the planet's cities

phosphorescing grids
where darkness adheres to the edges.

California Spring

We once lived on one side of Sutro Tower
under its radio waves,
facing the bay.

Now we live on the other side
where there is a zoo
and a sea.

Spring means
Sutro Tower's waist is obscured by fog.
Redwood doesn't grow mold in fog

so our house
like all these old houses
was built with it

from settler-felled forests
not far from here.
Painters painted that manifest desire

for a dream world
that doesn't erode, doesn't mold.
Their paintings hang in galleries few enter

preferring abstraction
but Bierstadt's
California Spring is there.

We live on this side of the country.
On the other side,
a court hands down a decision

and there is more suffering
reaching from there
to here.

They took oaths,
as we did, but we used rings
even though the future lacked certainty.

Sutro Tower looks brutal in the fog
with its body cut off.
Three legs without their instruments.

I've never been able to say we're doomed
though we've wiped out the bees —
not entirely,

but I haven't seen one for two years
until today,
which I know can't be true.

In Transit

The inflight copy of *Hemispheres*: "Three Perfect Days in Santa Barbara," which is exactly what we have, three days. Only from the air can we observe what's on the other side of California mountains, mountains that surround the Midway-Sunset oil field. A seemingly endless supply of oil beneath the ground we'll land on. It's easy to misunderstand where mountain and valley and desert begin and end. During the safety demonstration, he and I play a game. Unfolding the map in the back of *Hemispheres*, we point to locations where we want to fly to. We point to them, pretending to guess.

Blaze

Mulholland burns. Getty nudes
stand sentinel in ash.

Marie Antoinette's porcelain
lands in jeopardy a second time.

What a shame to watch
her lover's pillow burn.

From the hilltop museum,
it's difficult to tell

the city from a plywood empire
backed by buttresses.

I'm thinking about us,
how easily it could all become smoke.

I call you from the hotel
but don't mention that I was out late.

I tell you about the Watteau
with the lovers, the *innamorati*

who wear no masks. They're enchanted
by a guitar.

City Bees

But of all the embodiments ever built, I'd only return to one,
For the sexual New Jerusalem was by far the greatest fun.
    — Thom Gunn

People buy artisanal honey
     near the rainbow crosswalk.

Men are all working on balance
     inside a gym.

I translate a Swedish cookbook that says
     we should eat for Wellness.

If you don't use new vocabulary
     at least three times, it vanishes.

In the Castro, there are few reminders
     of those lost to AIDS–

the neighborhood funeral home
     where so many were brought

now shuttered and slated for condos.
     There was talk of a Trader Joe's.

Every week, lampposts are plastered
     with party posters

of boys in jockstraps.
     When I was young,

I feared I'd grow up and never
     be touched.

Starling Murmuration

Not a single nook of the helix fails to arc and coil over
the palm trees beside the hospital parking lot

as if they were drawn there by the breath of the underworld, the arm

of a radiation machine that only moments ago
aimed at my husband's brain.

A mesh mask kept him looking up at God

so the CyberKnife could leave
a small patch of skin where his beard no longer grows.

Whatever colorful deaths that machine delivered inside him,
he never bent a toe or twitched a finger.

Rotunda of birds–

how shipwrecked these starlings would be if just one froze.

Mariology

He pulls on his jeans
at the bed's edge,

notices my nightstand icon of the Virgin,
a bottle of poppers at her feet.

There's something forgettable
about both their faces.

He doesn't want to know
what omens feel like; angels should

just scatter when you're done risking.
Talisman propped against a lamp,

it was something I bought
for later in life.

I kept the lights on against his wishes,
so I could see ahead into our story.

Clothing Optional

Waiting for the inflatable dragon
to float my way,

I take a drag from a vape
offered to me by husbands

wearing caps with the word *Grrrr*.
Wading towards one another,

we share a spirit of unrestraint.
Legs dangling from the pool's edge,

a guy offers a drink from a random
bottle of tequila.

He seems proud to have found it,
so I take a sip.

It's the Fourth of July
and over a hundred degrees

beside this kidney-shaped pool
where people dance

in the water to the DJ
hired for the occasion,

while men go in and out of rooms
that look out onto the pool.

I don't go in the rooms,
just dance and watch

not celebrating anything specific
but a freedom to not care.

Election Night

On the dance floor,
my fingertip traces his infinity tattoo

and I wish more things were uncountable,
although cruelty is also endless.

A queen takes the stage, steeped in mimosa light,
beard glitter-dipped,

lip-syncs "Let the Sunshine In,"
a song I never realized was about heartbreak.

Its buoyant refrain can't save us.
In a poster over the bar,

Warhol's Marilyn scans the room
through antifreeze eyeshadow;

the guys look like they're
somewhere else too.

Cymbidium

Aren't I bothered that there are no seasons?
Don't I miss snow?

Arranged in ranks, you take care of yourselves:

bowl orchids,
cymbidium, yellow and red.

Unfatherly, I keep you outside.
You drink the fog,

papered in wet maple leaves
and cracked snail shells.

Cymbidium. Why would you want to be born now
on the eves of war

and impeachment?

From the window by my bed,
I can see the view:

the snowy alleyway, fire escapes.

If my orchids don't survive, then I'm not meant
to raise a child.

Rainbow Sprinkles Elegy

Because he can,
my brother eats an entire bowl of rainbow sprinkles
from the toppings bar. No ice cream.

The menu is a giant cow on the wall.

Sitting under its udder,
we try to salvage things.

We could also order mozzarella sticks,
which he does,
another thing about him that irritates me.

When he was younger,
he put his mouth under a candy dispenser
full of M&Ms.

They cascaded out of the store
and into the mall and just kept going.

Medications and special schools
have yet to break his impulse for pleasure.

Something urgent inside him
that none of us understand is about to detonate.
I still haven't even come out.

He sends me a letter from his boarding school
in Utah, and asks me
to send him AA batteries.

I have no idea what they're for.
He isn't allowed any electronics.

Interior Design

Mid-semester, my mother withdraws from college.
Gives me her translucent green templates.

One stencil is all circles,
so I draft a domed future.

Sea levels are only just starting to rise,
but something is gone for good.

It hasn't occurred to me yet that
it's exhausting to live in a bubble

or to scuttle a dream.
To cook for us and to clean us.

Just a child, I think only of coziness.
I make sure the domes are all touching.

It doesn't matter how we get inside them,
so I don't draw doors.

Beehive State Elegy

Hives emblazoned on temple doors and traffic signs,
this 45th state full of dinosaur bones.

Scientists can't find the bee graves either,
hidden in these mountains.

Nearby there's a ski lift
where a hundred years ago

people in cabins died young
like my brother.

We plant flowers in the median strip
near the spot he rolled his Jeep

while the 7-Eleven cashier watched
through bulletproof glass.

Only traces of him
remain in the desert, small as pollen,

which is what they find in mummy stomachs:
Ice Age flowers.

In Transit

Maybe the facts of what happened on a highway are not narrative facts in the way I was raised to think of time, but circular in that they always circle back to the same place, exit for some, entrance for others. In my family, a story existed and continues to exist. How my brother used to drive the freeway for hours in search of motorists to assist. We all have our theories as to why he drove his Jeep for hours in circles, never getting lost. On the Beltway, with its metaphorical human belly. Driving the Beltway, I realize how it holds things up or keeps them from falling.

Our Climate

Avenues of almond trees peaking. So-called valley snow.
The coast behind us—

we stop to eat at a Sizzler. Just a West Coast thing now.

The only two men seated together,
we talk about politicians and what we wanted and couldn't have.

Fidgeting with the rim of my baseball cap,
I'm glad I have it on.

The menu here makes everything so simple.

Along the 120, pallets of hives ready the orchards.
These trees use so much water.

Why grow something so hard to satisfy?

When this valley becomes desert,
almonds will seem short-lived.

Central Valley

I.

We pick pomegranates,
as many as we can carry,

our shirts held out like aprons.
This could be our utopia.

Can a pomegranate have
a front and a back?

I'm always facing you
in the wrong direction.

I've never even held
a pomegranate before;

its star-shaped mouth
says that it lived.

II.

Our fingers meet
in a bowl of soaking artichokes,

ants scatter through
my fingers.

I rest my hand
on the purple spikes.

The season's first artichoke weighed
almost nothing

like your head the first time
I ever cradled it

in my lap
after your radiation treatment.

I was afraid to change my posture,
to wake you.

Balloon Rapture

Eighteen thousand balloons
        dive into the Great Lakes,

some with handwritten notes
            from a Kansas elementary school–

I can see how those dreams
        would look like food to seabirds.

At the Party Store, my little sister's job
            was attaching mylar letters

to a helium canister's black-rubber beak.
        Consonants would spin in the wind,

spelling dissonant greetings.
            There isn't any logic

to why my parents release balloons
        on the anniversary

of my brother's death. If a balloon goes up,
        it comes down.

Christmas Elegy

Bound in twine
and last on the lot,

frozen and tubercular tree
against the fence.

A makeshift hotel Christmas,
brought to my brother,

unable to leave his reform school
for bad behavior.

Untied and left to thaw in the tub,
the tree burst overnight–

an evergreen heave,
evangelical in its

smell which filled the lobby
and almost got us kicked out.

We spent the night
looking at lights on mansions

in the Provo hills where
there were songs and warm babies.

Seahorse with Cotton Swab

after a photo by Justin Hofman

I snip clear rings
off a six-pack of tonic, swab

coffee table edges with a Q-tip
to get the crumbs out.

There must be a saint who died this way,

trying to polish
the inside of a wave.

New Year's Day
and the world is still unhealable.

This Q-tip may end up
in a viral video,

a seahorse clinging to it.

As the composition's
tallest element,

the Q-tip should represent heaven.

Stern Grove

Summer in Stern Grove amphitheater.

Coyotes live atop its wooded rim.

One got poor Bella the shih tzu.

They dig dens on Mt. Davidson under a giant cross.

It's in a scene from *Dirty Harry*.

In a YouTube video, a man points a gun at a coyote hole.

The cross used to light up at night.

FDR himself lit the lights all the way from Washington.

Vigilantes pledge law and order in convention speeches.

We bungee-cord the trash bins on Mondays.

A coyote stops to sniff them.

A deep scar says it has fought a rival.

I think of it curled in the chaparral under the cross

like a nativity scene from my childhood.

Tourists in Our Own City

Trying to position the Transamerica Pyramid
above our heads in a selfie.

What else are median strips for
but long kisses in front of buildings

we never saw being built?
Still, they bear names.

Coit Tower, Ferry Building.
A bus shudders by without stopping

because we're doing something obvious,
tourists in our own city. North Beach, our Little Italy,

a neighborhood within
a neighborhood. We buy

a Neapolitan cookie. He takes a bite
and hands me the other half.

Coastal Solitaire

On a Mendocino cliff

                three rusty links of a chain

                                dangle like a brooch

but just three.

        *

        He bends to touch the old anchor

as if this were the oracle.

                        It always tells us

                            to free the same thing.

                *

In these moments, I want him most.

        When he's reading

                or unwraps and offers me

                        a pinwheel peppermint.

                            *

            The ocean wears

                its platinum sweater.

Fall wind holds back the fog.

Sonoma

I.

Vines strung like telephone wire
to the tops of foothills

where grapes wait for fog to sweeten
them into vanilla and cherry.

A dog naps in the shade
of an olive tree and briefly looks up.

We have three pours made strong,
almost ink-black by the wood.

There are layers that don't even have names.
Nodding after a sip means you found one.

We pass *alfresco* gardens, the clink
of forks as people laugh

and touch each other on the shoulder
when they agree.

II.

Roman pines beside the pool
and nothing but the sound of guys diving

into the deep end.
The patter of their feet as they

walk dripping on the concrete,
their smooth wiry bodies

slipping beneath the water.
The cocktail we've been sharing

is mostly melted ice. When
he walks to the bar, I

watch the way almost
invisible hairs at the base

of his spine catch the sun.
Whatever he brings back,

I'll take a sip. I'm not
really reading.

III.

We walk the old town plaza.
Under a cottonwood tree, a picnic bench

covered with a SpongeBob tablecloth,
kids chasing one another.

A little girl in a party hat sits cross-legged
while a woman paints a butterfly

on her cheek. My mother takes a picture
and my father calls the girl *baby doll*.

My parents wave to her as I drive away,
off to our first tasting. My father

waits for us outside the winery.
He sits in a rocking chair

and watches a lizard investigate
a stone wall.

IV.

Next to General Vallejo's
bleached adobe barracks

silver SUVs park along Spain Street.
A single tree stands

in the dirt courtyard
where a small patch

of grass hasn't fully worn away.
My mother photographs

the empty wooden balcony
as if any moment someone

might throw open one
of those shuttered windows.

Desert Hymn

Too sweet,
oranges on the branch.

Wind in palms signals
a desert revising itself into dusk.

He climbs naked
from the pool

and water tries not to let go of him.

Hummingbirds skirmish
over blossoms whose

throats were made for them.
They live with a single craving,

to float in the desert air

like the mountain tram
we never ride.

Santa Cruz

He knows the highway exit
by heart,

his parents' new bungalow
near his childhood home.

They give us a box
of glass door knobs

they saved from the old house.
The pool is unheated

but warm from the blue tarp
that covers it overnight.

After swimming,
we find rocks to pin down

the tarp edges,
but the dogs are still curious.

One of them noses
under the greenhouse,

a crumbling folie
in the shape of a castle

built by the former owner
and now a hazard

like so much else.
We worry that his parents

will fall here. His dad gives
us a book he says is too long

for him to remember.
Under the greenhouse,

the dog's face is covered
in wild fennel pollen.

In Transit

How had I gotten from there to here: there, as always, was the question.
— Joan Didion

I want to tell you what I remember photographing from the air. The photos remain but not the memories of why I wanted pictures at that altitude, the wing intruding on half of them, a meaning only fully understood from that godlike vantage. I question belief in God, though the preflight ritual is one of the few times I feel the desire for faith, at the mercy of forces but also the precise decisions of the ground crew tending to the impossible concept of human flight. As the cabin door closes, I receive a push notification that my bag is on board somewhere below us along with mail whose final destination is not my destination.

Nurse Plant

It will outgrow its nurse,
but until then,
the young saguaro
enjoys the shade
of a mesquite tree.
The mesquite has long roots
that bring water
close enough
for the young saguaro
to drink.
The saguaro doesn't thrive
in Palm Springs,
but there is a resort
called The Saguaro
where we sip
bottomless mimosas.
One summer,
a man drowned
in The Saguaro's party pool
while everyone danced.
We were there
that summer,
but we had our own pool.
Humans pump so much water
we tilted the earth,
a headline declares.
Our Airbnb has controls
to keep our pool
from overheating
or its lights from cycling
an endless LED rainbow.
The host is particular
about these measures
posted on the refrigerator
under a magnet shaped

like a martini.
When we dare to lower
the thermostat to its lowest
setting anyway,
our wet feet tiptoe
on cold porcelain tile.

Seismic Wave

Tonight I sleep with my cheek on the cool concrete
by the black luggage tracks
while my summer flu takes hold.
Walls, ceiling, and floor
all painted the same glossy white,
a vacation rental with no edges.
Two all-night Pride parties
caught up with me,
and in my fever, my forehead pressed to the floor,
I think I hear
a tremor.
The next day, a nurse at Desert Regional will inform me
that there was a quake
north of Joshua Tree
while she straps a pink armband on my wrist.
How will I explain what could only be
described as supernatural
lying there with my cheek against the cool floor.
Not just a baring of my soul
or promises not to be so drunk I accept
an Afrin bottle with no label
from a dance floor stranger – no,
tonight, my forehead is against the floor
and I hear something
or someone
whose only message during the first wave
is that there will be a second one.

Celestial Elegy

Blue shoe booties in a box
at the temple entrance.
We're non-believers.
There's so much carpet.

Walls anointed
a shade of insulin.
Before entering,
all visitors watch a video

about becoming a Mormon family.
A boarding school here might
make my brother
follow directions

or stand still
like the teenager
with shiny teeth
holding the box for discarded booties.

The tour ends
after the Celestial Room,
the closest you can get
to being off-planet

but my family will not convert.
An Elder suspects
my brother attends services
for the donuts.

The Fish

The next table claps
when our order arrives:
whole fish baked in sea salt.
With the side
of a serving spoon,
the waiter cracks
the crust open.
Even its eyes
are shrouded in salt.
Each person gets a mouthful.
It's the fleeing that
makes it tender.
I can't be sure I've
ever loved anything this whole,
that I'll ever be this close again
to something so expensive.
Hot Santa Ana wind mopes
across clay courts–
cigarette ash drops
from the balcony.
My view includes
the hotel loading dock:
a catering truck unloads
clean, bone-colored napkins.

Portfolio

A hotel's portfolio expands,
a boutique property
with signature restaurant
(subject to finalizing
a new management agreement)

a few blocks north
of the new Cultural Museum
for the Agua Caliente
Band of Cahuilla Indians
whose land this is. First an Andaz,

now another chain,
on one of the checkerboard
tribal allotments divided when
the first railroad to Yuma
came through town.

One hundred and sixty-four luxury guest rooms
built by a Dallas-based developer,
each with mountain views.
(For now, three hundred industrial lights
on orange electrical cords illuminate

prefab blocks that will become suites
if the financing goes through.)
Amenities include indoor
and outdoor bars and lounges,
six thousand square feet of event space

and high-end street-level retail.
Curated food and beverage
plus "community engagement"
and "benefits." A saltwater pool
that holds one hundred and twenty thousand gallons

(as much as a desert storm drain).
Endless water across multiple pools.
A new company's take on Lifestyle.
Rooms are no longer
rooms, they're bungalows.

Tattoo

This Marriott in the foothills
has a heated indoor pool

empty on a December weeknight,
no lifeguard on duty.

My husband sips a beer
we snuck past the lobby.

He wants to get the tattoo
he's been planning since

his remission:
the radiation symbol

with its yellow and black
fan blades. Right on his shoulder.

A lot of skin
I think I should have a say over.

Would I ever get one?
He knows what I'll say.

Something discreet,
on an ankle,

a sleeve tat maybe
inside the biceps

but one where the phrase
disappears inside the shirt cuff.

Single Sheet

A bedroom fan
on its highest setting
wobbling–

when you wake me,
I know
what you want.

There could be things
more dear
to us right now:

water, A/C.
But we can give
them away for a morning

as you say nothing,
moving your mouth
down my chest.

Outdoor Shower

made of glass
breezeblocks.
Each of us

has a towel
our host rolled
and tucked in a basket

by the front door.
On the back
of a postcard, he wrote

Welcome! So many
have been welcomed here.
Everything arranged

to make us powerless
to sun, to seek relief.
But I won't give you that,

even alone together
in the cooling shower,
positioned behind you,

your body pressed
against the glass blocks,
unseen but also seen.

Everything feels excruciatingly close–
even hummingbirds–
when you're half transparent,

a nude blur.

Three Views of L.A.

Mormon Temple

In the visitors' center,
lost things are real:
a room with painted, fiberglass stones
and oil lamps,
a stylized Biblical dwelling
meant to transport me
to ancient places.
I push a button
that lights up historic sites
on a map.
Something else is there now.
I can see the temple spires
from my hotel,
its grounds as manicured
as any studio backlot.
I think about what I've dedicated
my life to,
in L.A., killing time
before my conference paper
on films no one
this side of the Atlantic
will see.

Getty Museum

In the tram ascending
burnt hillside,
I see Bel Air pools
in the canyon below.
The museum's contributions
have weathered
criticism, fire.
Its stone pavilions
are surrounded
by fountain-fed moats.
From here,
it's the kind of view
that makes me imagine
not going home,
but not staying here.
Too bad.
I wanted inspiration.
To receive
a passionate poem
in my mind.

Studio Visit

The crowd warms up
between scenes
on a soundstage with a thousand
overhead lights.
I pose for a photo
in the high school hallway set
with friends who are writers
also called Co-Executive Producers.
I skip the conference dinner
to sit in my first
green room.
The show's principal characters
are younger than us,
a show about somewhere else
in America.
It takes so many overhead lights
to simulate sunshine.

Survival

Under the gilded wooden beams
of the throwback lounge,

the waiter says the Roosevelt Hotel
is haunted.

A favorite of Marilyn's,
hers is not the only ghost.

My cocktail comes with smoke,
advertised as classic,

like the hotel's neon sign
a landmark.

Everything on Sunset
is a landmark at least once.

The smoke shop that
sells Dunhills

in the red rectangular box
used to be a place

people recognized.
It's astonishing any of these things last.

For our tenth year,
we have dinner at the Roosevelt

beside the Hockney pool,
its blue squiggles

hand-painted by the artist,
each one recently restored.

Desert Ride

I need cigarettes.

In the scorching sun,

my body asks for unorthodox things.

I'll never get enough of him,

tank top, back tat, walking inside for booze

and a crisp copy of *Architectural Digest*

that smells like propane,

pages filled with celebrity pools.

Along the highway,

planes time their landings.

Windows down,

radio turned up,

everyone's song of summer

is about addiction and love.

Bees in the Maraschino Cherry Factory

Red frenzy,
honey the taste of cough syrup

or a medicine
that could save you.

These bees are greedy to taste,
the world aphrodisiacal.

They're dancing differently–

after all, it's a red world now,
feverish and fiery,

which is how the present feels.

San Francisco is too cold
for many flowers,

but like those bloodshot bees,
we moved to this place

to create a custom-made life.

Though death followed us
here, too.

Best then to end on ecstasy,

to have stepped way off balance
like bees unprepared

for the rush
their legs shaped.

Notes

"But of all the embodiments ever built, I'd only return to one, / For the sexual New Jerusalem was by far the greatest fun" is quoted from Thom Gunn's "Jokes, etc." and from his collection *Boss Cupid*.

"Balloon Rapture" was inspired by an article published online in the *Detroit Free Press* entitled "18,000 pieces of balloon waste were found in Great Lakes: Why it's a danger," written by Keith Matheny and published on June 17, 2019.

"Seahorse with Cotton Swab" was inspired by a photo taken by Justin Hofman in 2017.

"How had I gotten from there to here: there, as always, was the question" is quoted from *South and West* by Joan Didion.

"Bees in the Maraschino Cherry Factory" was inspired by an article in the *New York Times* entitled "The Mystery of the Red Bees of Red Hook" written by Susan Dominus and published on November 29, 2010.

Acknowledgments

My gratitude to the editors of the following journals in which these poems first appeared, sometimes in previous versions:

Poem-a-Day (*Academy of American Poets*): "Palm Springs"
The American Poetry Review: "Blaze," "Balloon Rapture," "City Bees," and "Seahorse with Cotton Swab"
Cherry Tree: "Beehive State Elegy"
Couplet Poetry: "Bees in the Maraschino Cherry Factory"
Hobart: "Election Night" and "Mariology"
The Kenyon Review: "California Spring" and "Quake"
Los Angeles Review: "Airbnb Art"
Meridian: "Starling Murmuration"
Pleiades: "Gadolinium (Gd)"
Poetry Northwest: "The Fish"
The Yale Review: "Mid-Century Modern"

Endless gratitude to Steve Bellin-Oka for selecting my manuscript and to Kris Bigalk and to Matt Mauch at Trio House Press. Working with editors David Groff and Natasha Kane was a gift.

There isn't a way to fully express how much my friendship with Richie Hofmann has made every poem in this book better.

Profound thanks to Diane Seuss for believing in my work and for such generosity. To my first poetry teacher, Robert Farnsworth, who inspired me. To Henri Cole, who always told me to "keep going."

I'm grateful for so many people whose support sustained me in some way while I wrote this book: William Brewer, Ryann Stevenson, Noah Warren, Aria Aber, Brian Tierney, Jess Eagle, Armen Davoudian, Randall Mann, Fatima Kola, Katie Peterson, Derrick Austin, James Longenbach, Alexander Chee, Jenny Johnson, Mark Bibbins, Stephen Guy-Bray, Spencer Reece, Maggie Millner, Mark Wunderlich, Elizabeth Scanlon, Sam Bett, Todd Portnowitz, Keith

Ekiss, Kellam Ayres, Ginger Murchison, Laura Van Prooyen, Annie Schumacher, Amy Stewart, Johnnie Thompson, Ian Hunter, Paula Williamson, Nikkole Gadsden, Ricardo Lima, Jeff Ramsey, Sabina Ivenäs, Joakim Olsson, Claes Ljunghorn, Lotta Håkans, Tobias Helgesson, Erik Nordman, Rui Tian, Antoinette Kenmuir-Evans, Leo Chu, Eric Garcia, Robert Berman, Chase Brock, Ann Percival, Ed Victor, Evan Smith, Brian Woolf, and Amy Webb.

For generous financial support during the creation of this book, I want to thank the Bread Loaf Writers' Conference and the Kenyon Review Writing Workshops. Thanks to Jennifer Grotz, David Baker, and Nicole Terez Dutton for their faith in my work.

To the Gullette, Stevens, Wells, Lloyd, and Weaver families, thank you for your unfailing support.

Thanks to my parents and my sister Meghan, who cheered me on.

Love to Michael Stevens, for always believing.

And in memory of my brother. Jeremy, this is also for you.

About the Author

Christian Gullette's poems have appeared in *The American Poetry Review*, *Kenyon Review*, the *Poem-a-Day* (*Academy of American Poets*), and *The Yale Review*. He has received financial support from the Bread Loaf Writers' Conference and the Kenyon Review Writers Workshops. Christian completed his Ph.D. in Scandinavian Languages and Literatures at the University of California, Berkeley, and when not serving as the editor-in-chief of *The Cortland Review*, he works as a lecturer and translator. He lives in San Francisco.

ABOUT THE BOOK

Coachella Elegy was designed at Trio House Press through the collaboration of:

David Groff, Lead Editor
Natasha Kane, Supporting Editor and Interior Design
Joel W. Coggins, Cover Design

The text is set in Adobe Caslon Pro.

ABOUT THE PRESS

Trio House Press is an independent literary press dedicated to discovering, publishing, and promoting books that enhance culture and the human experience. Trio House Press adheres to and supports all ethical standards and guidelines outlined by the CLMP. For further information, or to consider making a donation to Trio House Press, visit us online at triohousepress.org.

Printed in the USA
CPSIA information can be obtained
at www.ICGtesting.com
CBHW031333190224
4446CB00005B/23